SandCastle™
Primeros Sonidos

Sierra y Morris

Cathy Camarena, M.Ed., and Gloria B. Ruff, M.Ed.

Consulting Editors
Lourdes Flores-Hanson, M.S.E., and Gloria Rosso-White

ABDO Publishing Company

capstone
www.capstoneclassroom.com

Credits
Curriculum Coordinator: Nancy Tuminelly
Cover and Interior Design and Production: Mighty Media
Child Photography: Steven Wewerka, Wewerka Photography
Photo Credits: AbleStock, Comstock, Tracy Kompelien, Photodisc

ISBN 978-1-4966-0369-2 (paperback)

Printed in the United States of America in North Mankato, Minnesota.
032019 001726

SandCastle™ books are created by a professional team of educators, reading specialists, and content developers around five essential components that include phonemic awareness, phonics, vocabulary, text comprehension, and fluency. All books are written, reviewed, and leveled for guided and early intervention reading, and designed for use in shared, guided, and independent reading and writing activities to support a balanced approach to literacy instruction.

SandCastle Level: Beginning

rr

ABCChDEFGH
IJKLLLMNÑOP
QRSTUVWXYZ

abcchdefgh
ijklllmnñop
qrstuvwxyz

Sierra

Morris

churros

torre

parrilla

perro

carro

Vemos los .

Vemos la  .

Vemos la  .

Vemos el .

Vemos el  .

A Sierra le gusta el perro.

El perro es pequeño.

A Morris le gustan los churros.

Los churros son dulces.

Al perro le gustan los churros.

¿Cuáles de estas cosas contienen rr?

Más palabras que contienen rr

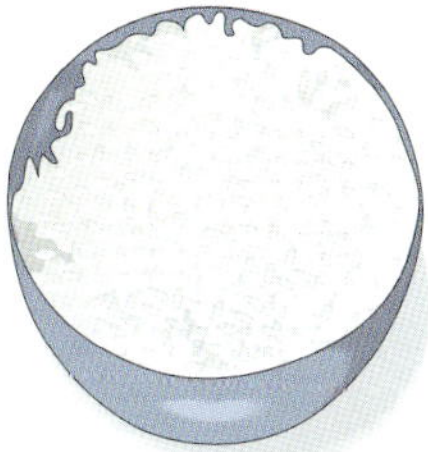

arroz

burro

carreta

gorra

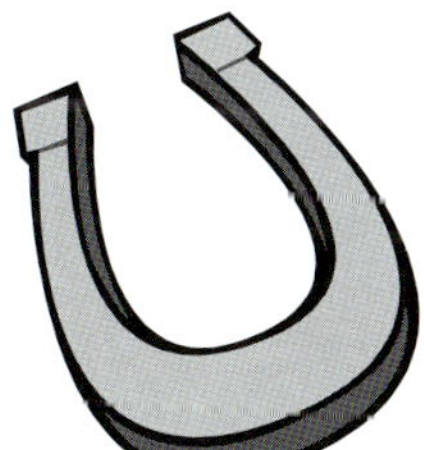

herradura

About SandCastle™

A professional team of educators, reading specialists, and content developers created the SandCastle™ series to support young readers as they develop reading skills and strategies and increase their general knowledge. The SandCastle™ series has four levels that correspond to early literacy development in young children. The levels are provided to help teachers and parents select the appropriate books for young readers.

Emerging Readers
(no flags)

Beginning Readers
(1 flag)

Transitional Readers
(2 flags)

Fluent Readers
(3 flags)

These levels are meant only as a guide. All levels are subject to change.

ABDO Publishing Company
www.abdopub.com

capstone®
www.capstoneclassroom.com